THE SEA WORLD BOOK OF
PENGUINS

TEXT AND PHOTOGRAPHS
BY FRANK S. TODD

A Sea World Book for Young Readers

Sea World Press
1250 South Avenue, San Diego, CA 92101

HARCOURT BRACE JOVANOVICH
New York and London

THE SEA WORLD BOOK OF PENGUINS

Text and photographs by Frank S. Todd
Editorial direction by Cynthia Edwards
Design by Carla Clarke

 A Sea World Press Publication

**Library of Congress
Cataloging in Publication Data**

Todd, Frank S.
  The Sea World book of penguins.

  (Sea World book for young readers)

  Bibliography: p.
  Includes index.
  SUMMARY: Describes the physical
characteristics, habits, and behavior of
various species of penguins.
  1. Penguins—Juvenile literature.
[1. Penguins] I. Title. II. Series.
QL696.S473T62 1981
    598.4'41   80-25588
ISBN 0-15-004040-7

First Edition

A B C D E

Additional photography credits

Ken Fink: pg. 77
Robert French, Sea World, Inc.: pg. 86-top
Mike Helms, USN (VXE-6/Helos):
pg. 11-top
Jerry Roberts, Sea World, Inc.:
pg. 15-lower right
Smithsonian Institution Photo No. 74-1570:
pg. 11-middle
Ralph and B. J. Schreiber: pg. 76
John Warham: pgs. 58-59, 67, 69

Author's acknowledgements

Most of the initial penguin field work was
supported by the National Science
Foundation (Office of Polar Programs). I
gratefully acknowledge their assistance.
The role of George Llano, Chief Scientist
(retired) cannot be minimized. The
enthusiastic Navy helicopter pilots of
Squadron VXE-6 deserve special
recognition. In recent years, T.C. Swartz of
Society Expeditions, and the International
Foundation for the Conservation of Birds
have been particularly helpful. The
success achieved with the penguins at
Sea World is a tribute to the skill and
dedication of my superb aviculture staff.

First page photograph: A group of Adelie penguins in front of a glacier.

Title page photograph: A small section of a macaroni penguin rookery.

Following page photograph: An emperor penguin exploding from the sea onto the ice edge.

CONTENTS

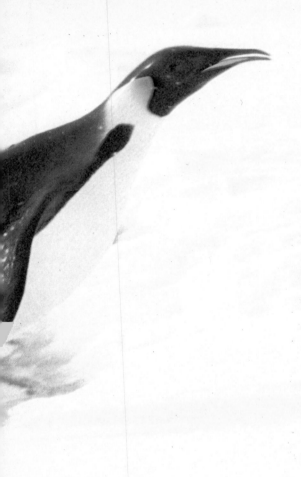

Dedicated to penguin
lovers everywhere —
young and old alike.

AN INTRODUCTION
CHAPTER ONE

People everywhere know what a penguin is; or at least they think they do. Penguins are continually referred to as inquisitive little men dressed up in tuxedos, with no place to go. I once heard an excited tourist remark, after seeing a huge group of penguins, that the scene brought to mind a headwaiters' convention.

Undoubtedly, it is the penguins' upright stance and their "formal attire" that has made them so fascinating to humans. No other animal is so often pictured in cartoons. To people the world over, penguins are considered almost human.

Penguins are so appealing that they consistently rank

among the top ten "must see" zoo animals. For some strange reason, boldly patterned black-and-white animals have always been intriguing. The giant panda, for example, is an all-time zoo favorite. And, in recent years, the killer whale has captured the hearts of many. Like the penguins, both of these animals are so distinctly patterned black and white that they appear hand-painted.

Our attachment to penguins is clear enough. But what do you suppose the penguins think about us? The noted penguin specialist Bernard Stonehouse perhaps stated it best when he said: "I have often had the impression that, to penguins, man is just another penguin — different, less predictable, occasionally violent, but tolerable company when he sits still and minds his own business."

There may be more misconceptions about penguins than about any other animal. Many people are even surprised to learn that penguins are birds. Some refuse to believe it, even after they have been told. I am often asked how the penguins' "fur" remains so sleek. (Penguins do not have fur; they have feathers.) Or, if Eskimos really eat penguins. (Eskimos live in the Arctic where there are no penguins.) I have even been asked how penguins can survive at the South Pole. (They don't. The South Pole is at least eight hundred miles from the nearest water and is approximately ten thousand feet in altitude.) And I frequently hear that "penguins are so cute and cuddly, they obviously would make wonderful pets." Not so. In fact, nothing could be further from the truth.

What, then, is a penguin? Penguins are stocky, flightless seabirds, with short, stout legs. They are not mammals or "feathered fish." They do not have fur like a dog or bare smooth skin like a porpoise. Their sleek outer covering consists of feathers. Penguins share a number of characteristics with other groups of animals, but they are birds, and birds alone have feathers.

All penguins live in the Southern Hemisphere. No penguins, past or present, have ever naturally ranged north of the equator. Penguins traditionally have been symbolic of the Antarctic. However, only *two* of the seventeen species of penguins are restricted to that freezing continent. In fact, one species lives in the enchanted isles of the Galapagos, almost astride the equator.

Penguins are unquestionably unique and exotic birds. At least 8800 species of birds are known to exist today. But penguins are so distinctive in appearance and behavior that they are almost never confused with any other bird — or, for that matter, any other animal.

Previous page: Adelie penguins find the footing slippery on the slick ice. There can be no question that penguins are addictive, but as one biologist cleverly noted, the addiction is fortunately not dangerous to the health of the observer.

Above: A killer whale in the Antarctic surveying its surroundings.

Middle: A giant panda in the snow.

Below: A pair of Adelie penguins at their nest site.

ORIGIN AND DISCOVERY
CHAPTER TWO

Although penguins cannot fly today, they evolved from flying birds. Nevertheless, the fossil record suggests that penguins have remained essentially unchanged in form for forty million years or more.

The first penguin fossil was found in New Zealand in the mid 1800's. Since that time, the bones of many now extinct species have been discovered. Most of these extinct penguins were about the size of penguins existing today. But two species were enormous: they stood over five feet in height and could possibly have weighed as much as three hundred pounds. The largest penguin living today is the emperor penguin, a magnif-

icent bird, which stands about three and a half feet tall and weighs up to ninety pounds. In contrast, the smallest penguin — the fairy penguin — is only a little over a foot tall and weighs merely two and a half pounds. It is smaller even than any of the extinct penguins.

How did the penguin get its name? Curiously, the birds that we know as penguins today were not the first animals to be called penguins. As explorers began to sail into the north Atlantic Ocean, they discovered a large black-and-white flightless bird. They called this bird the penguin. But today it is better known as the great auk. Then, as the early mariners became

Previous page: Magellanic penguins. Penguins have no close surviving relatives, but they appear to be most closely related to the albatross and the petrels. This is ironic because while penguins are flightless, the albatross is one of the most accomplished of all fliers.

Above: Two emperor penguins. These birds are the largest and most majestic of the 17 species of penguins.

Right: Even as adults, fairy penguins are dwarfed by their human companion.

Opposite page:

Left: Murres are strikingly similar to penguins in appearance. However, unlike the flightless penguins, murres can fly.

Upper right: A tufted puffin in flight.

Lower right: A puffin underwater with a fish.

more daring and began to venture farther and farther south, the true penguins were eventually encountered. Because they looked so much like the great auks (which at that time were called penguins), the name was naturally applied to the southern birds as well.

No one really knows the origins of the name penguin. Some historians indicate the name may have been derived from the Welsh words *pen gwyn*, roughly meaning white head. Great auks did not have white heads, but they did have a large white spot on the head. Others suggest the name originated from the Latin word *pinguis*, perhaps referring to the fat, or blubber of the bird.

The great auk was a member of the group of birds known as alcids. Other alcids include the puffins, murres, and auklets. All these birds live in the Northern Hemisphere. And all surviving alcids can fly — both through the air and underwater. While alcids and penguins are somewhat alike in appearance

and lifestyle, they are not closely related.

Considering its original name, it is not surprising that the flightless great auk was the most penguin-like of the alcids. The great auk stood some thirty inches tall and weighed ten to sixteen pounds, the same size as the medium-sized penguins. Tragically, the great auk (and its eggs) was considered good eating. As a result, these defenseless, trusting birds were slaughtered in countless numbers. Finally, in June of 1844, the last of the magnificent great auks was massacred. Its memory lives on, but it is a miserable substitute for the real thing.

The true penguins were unknown to Europeans until at least the 1480's. At that time, it is believed that the South African black-footed penguin was seen by early Portuguese navigators. But this early contact was not documented. Therefore, historians generally credit the expedition of Ferdinand Magellan with seeing penguins for the first time — about 1520. The species sighted became known as the Magellanic penguin in honor of the famous explorer.

There are seventeen different species of penguins. These seventeen species make up six groups. One of the most distinctive groups consists of the brush-tailed, or long-tailed, penguins. The Adelies, gentoos, and chinstraps constitute this group. The two largest penguins, the emperor and king, are the most majestic of the penguins. Together they form another group. The six species of crested penguins are all quite similar in appearance and make up yet another group. Likewise, the four species of warm-weather penguins cannot be confused with any of the other penguins. The yellow-eyed and fairy penguins are each distinctive enough to be considered separately. However, in this book, these species are described together in chapter seven.

Most penguin species are easily distinguishable. A few, however, such as the fairy, gentoo, and rockhopper, have been further divided into subspecies. Experts do not always agree on classification. However, for the penguin lover the complexities of classification are of little concern. The penguins themselves know who they are. And, as the various penguins are described in the chapters ahead, you too will know who they are.

Largest of the alcids, the great auk was the first bird to be known as a penguin. Like the true penguins, it was flightless — a condition which no doubt hurried its extinction.

Below: The Magellanic penguin was one of the first penguins to be seen by the adventurous European seafarers.

THE
REMARKABLE PENGUIN
CHAPTER THREE

Penguins live throughout the Southern Hemisphere along many coastlines and in many different climates. It is true that several species are very much at home in the freezing Antarctic, the most southern place on the globe, but most penguins favor the warmer, more northerly, isolated subantarctic islands. And some also live along the coasts of South America, South Africa, Australia, and New Zealand — including even the tropical Galapagos Islands.

Penguins generally inhabit regions that are free of land predators. If they were in the Arctic, the flightless penguins would be defenseless against powerful Arctic predators such as polar

bears and cunning Arctic foxes. On the other hand, some flight-less birds, such as the ostrich, can survive in association with predatory lions and leopards because of their size and speed. Penguins do not have that advantage.

Since land predators do not occur in most places where penguins live, penguins are essentially fearless when ashore. On land, most species exhibit little fear of humans. Indeed, many penguins can be rather inquisitive and may even walk right up to closely inspect a human visitor. Some biologists suggest this may be because penguins are rather nearsighted. Their vision is better suited to water than air. Their curiosity may sometimes get the better of them; I have even had penguins stroll into my field tent to investigate.

Penguins are by far the most aquatic of all birds. Some species spend up to seventy-five percent of their lives in the sea, coming ashore only to breed and molt. Migratory penguins may remain at sea for three to five months at a time, although they occasionally rest on ice floes. On the other hand, tropical species, such as the Galapagos penguin, do not migrate and probably come ashore daily.

Because so much of their time is spent in the water, penguins have evolved to the point that they are ideally suited to an aquatic environment. Since it is impossible to be perfectly designed for both a water and land existence, it is easy to understand why they are somewhat uncomfortable when they are ashore. In other words, when they are on land they are out of their element.

However, even then, penguins are far from helpless. A penguin can move as fast, or faster, over soft snow than a human can run. And, they are very efficient tobogganers. The pingpong-like jumps of the rockhopper penguin require much coordination. And some penguins are excellent climbers. It is just that penguins are not as graceful when walking as they are

when swimming.

Although safe ashore, penguins are not always safe in the water. They must be constantly alert when swimming, or aquatic predators such as leopard seals, killer whales, fur seals, sea lions, and possibly sharks will quickly make a meal of them. In some regions, even octopus may be a threat.

Fortunately, penguins are far from helpless when in the water. They are superb swimmers, and their underwater maneuverability is almost beyond belief. Their wings have become

Previous page: Emperor penguins tobogganing.

Opposite page: Inquisitive Adelie penguins.

Above: As long as these Adelies remain on the ice, they are safe from the hungry leopard seal.

Left: A leopard seal smashing through thin ice in pursuit of a panicky Adelie penguin.

modified into powerful, flattened, paddle-like flippers. They can't be folded like a typical bird wing; thus movement is only possible at the shoulder. These long and narrow flippers enable penguins to swim at speeds of ten to fifteen miles per hour. Their feet and tails do not add power, but aid in steering.

Penguins breathe by leaping out of the water while swimming at top speed and gulping a breath of air. During this time, they look very much like jumping porpoises. So, this behavior is known as porpoising.

Although penguins cannot fly through the air, they definitely "fly" underwater. They do not have hollow bones. Hollow bones benefit a flying bird by reducing its weight, but they are not needed for a nonflier. In fact, their solid, heavier bones make penguins less buoyant and help them when diving.

Penguins are well known for their streamlined bodies. Because water is more dense than air, a great deal of energy is required to propel an object through it. The penguins' torpedo shape greatly reduces drag and increases their efficiency underwater.

Unfortunately, we know very little about the life of the penguin when it is at sea. However, it is known that the emperor penguin can dive to a depth of almost nine hundred feet; and it

The sleek-streamlined shape of this young Humboldt penguin is typical of all penguin species.

can stay under for almost twenty minutes. This is a remarkable feat for a bird. In fact, no other bird can come close to matching the penguin underwater.

Penguins, like all birds and mammals, are warm-blooded.* Therefore, they must maintain a constant body temperature, regardless of the external temperature. This presents some problems. All penguins, whether they live along the frigid coasts of Antarctica or the tropics of Galapagos, need to regulate their body temperature. The temperature extremes are mind boggling, ranging from 80°F below zero during the Antarctic winter to +100°F along the equator. No other group of

Left: A pair of porpoising Adelie penguins.

Below: A large school of porpoising penguins resembles a rain storm racing over the surface of the water.

*The body temperature of most penguins ranges between 100 and 102°F. This is lower than the temperature of most birds, but higher than that of most mammals. Humans, for example, maintain a body temperature of 98.6°F.

birds is forced to face such temperature extremes. The polar penguins must conserve heat. In contrast, the penguins in the warm northern regions must shed excess heat.

The cold-weather penguins are well insulated. They have a thick layer of blubber and are well feathered. In some cases, even much of their bill is feathered. The only bare skin that is exposed is on their feet. As a rule, a larger animal is more resistent to freezing temperatures than a smaller one. So, it is not surprising that the largest of the penguins, the emperor, lives in the coldest environment. Nevertheless, strange as it may seem , even the Antarctic species sometimes overheat; especially the dark, downy chicks.

The warm-climate penguins have exposed areas of pinkish skin on their faces. In addition, they have large bare legs and feet. When these penguins become overheated, the warm blood flows to the surface. The excess heat is transferred to the air when it reaches the bare skin areas. This cools the penguin down. The system works very much like a car radiator.

At times, penguins may also fluff up feathers to allow hot air to escape. Or, they may pant, just as a dog pants when it overheats. When the temperature becomes too hot, some penguins spend the day underground in burrows, where it is cooler.

A protesting Magellanic penguin at the entrance of its burrow. The bare facial skin helps this penguin regulate its body temperature. Note the backward-pointing spiny projections on the roof of the mouth and tongue. These help to direct food down the throat.

And even the most tropical penguins live in areas that have constant cool-water currents.

As we said in chapter one, the penguins' slick outer covering consists of feathers. Penguins have more feathers than do typical birds. Incredibly, seventy feathers or more can be found per square inch. These shiny feathers are quite long and stiff. They are all relatively uniform in size and shape. Each is somewhat curved, and overlaps its neighbor, like scales or tiles on a roof. This overlapping design is what keeps penguins waterproof.

The feathers must be cared for, or preened, often. Preening is necessary the same way that combing one's hair is necessary. Like all aquatic birds, penguins have a well-developed preen or oil gland. This special gland is located at the base of the tail and is used to keep the feathers well oiled. Obviously, the feathers must be well oiled if they are to remain waterproof.

Penguin feathers wear out after about a year. Therefore, they must be replaced. Think of feathers as a suit of clothes. Sooner or later, new ones are required. With birds, the process of shedding the old feathers and growing new ones is known as molting.

Molting penguins are faced with a number of problems.

An Adelie penguin gathering oil from its preen gland, which can be seen at the base of the tail. The oil, when spread over the feathers during preening, helps keep the penguin waterproof. (A penguin that is not waterproof stands little chance of survival in the freezing waters of the Antarctic.)

Since they live in a cold-water environment, they cannot afford to molt a little bit at a time, like most birds. If they did, they would no longer be waterproof and could become chilled and die. So they molt all the feathers at once. The new feathers grow in under the old ones and push them out, making the molting penguins look very bedraggled.

And, to make matters worse, since they are obviously not waterproof during the molt, they cannot go into the sea. Therefore, they cannot feed. This period of not eating is called fasting. When fasting, penguins depend on their layer of blubber for nourishment. As a result, they may lose twenty to thirty percent of their body weight. The entire process usually takes about thirty days. Most penguins molt on land, but Adelie and emperor penguins may molt on drifting ice floes at sea.

One thing that practically everyone knows about penguins is that they are usually seen in the company of great numbers of other penguins. In the case of most penguins, numbers is the name of the game. In fact, literally millions of penguins can be found in some breeding areas, or rookeries, as they are called. A large, active rookery brings to mind a busy beehive. The spectacle must be seen to be believed and appreciated. Some colonies are so enormous that they are heard, and smelled, long before they are seen. Larger rookeries can cover hundreds of acres.

Penguins even gather in large numbers when entering the water. Some species tend to mass together at favored jumping-off sites. There is an oft-repeated tale stating that when a group of Adelie penguins assembles at the water's edge, one

Opposite page: A molting gentoo penguin. During the molt, feathers fall from the birds like leaves from a deciduous tree at the approach of winter. This task is very demanding and requires a great deal of energy. Molting penguins may lose thirty percent of their body weight.

Upper left: Adelie penguins jumping from an ice edge.

Lower left: Adelie penguins are less graceful when they enter the water from a sloping rocky shore.

is pushed in by its fellow penguins to determine if dangerous leopard seals are present. If the "sacrifice victim" is not eaten, the other penguins will follow. Like most myths, this is an interesting tale, but not true. However, sometimes the pressure of the crowding penguins may actually force those birds nearest the water's edge in. The others usually follow immediately.

Since penguins live in such a variety of habitats, their techniques of getting out of the water vary. In areas with flat beaches, the penguins simply ride in on the surf and walk ashore, or are unceremoniously tossed up on the beach by the pounding breakers. Some climb or jump out on the rocks.

However, in the Antarctic, the shoreline may be covered by a wall of ice. So the Adelie penguins swim rapidly toward shore and when they reach the ice edge, pop out of the water like guided missiles. This method is also effective when a penguin wants to hop aboard an ice floe or iceberg. It is particularly efficient when a hungry leopard seal is in hot pursuit. Penguins usually jump vertically three to four feet, but leaps of more than six feet have been observed. They sometimes miss altogether or smash against the ice, and their landings are not always graceful.

Opposite page and above: Popping from the water to the ice edge above is usually done with grace and style . . . but not always!

Penguins feed on a variety of organisms. However, their favorite food consists of fish, krill, and squid, which they catch and eat underwater. Krill is a shrimp-like crustacean that is extremely abundant in cold southern waters. Krill is the steady diet of countless marine animals. Even the mighty blue whale depends primarily on it for its existence.

Penguins nest in a variety of ways. Some construct stone nests; others use vegetation. Some burrow underground. And the king and emperor penguins build no nests at all: their eggs are incubated on the tops of their feet. Depending on the species, one or two eggs are laid, rarely three. The eggs vary in color from white to bluish or greenish, but are not patterned.

The time required for the eggs to hatch is known as the incubation period. This ranges between thirty-two and sixty-four days. In all but one case, both male and female penguins incubate. During incubation, the eggs are held close to a featherless area on the belly. This warm bare skin is known as

the brood patch.

When hatching begins, the chicks first "pip" by poking a small hole in the egg. The chicks are calling loudly at this time. It is believed that the parents are already beginning to recognize the specific calls of their own chicks. Once the egg is pipped, the chick rotates within the egg, chipping the eggshell away as it turns. Finally, the top of the egg is pushed off, and the exhausted baby penguin emerges.

The newly hatched chicks are covered with down and are totally dependent on their attentive parents for survival. Penguin chicks are fed partially digested food. The feeding adults pass up food from their stomachs in a process known as regurgitation.

Once a chick reaches the point of being fully feathered, it is on its own. At this stage, it has fledged. Fledging periods are also variable; as short as seven weeks for an Adelie chick or up to thirteen months for a king penguin chick.

Opposite page, left: A king penguin incubating an egg. The egg is balanced on the top of this dutiful parent's feet.

Opposite page, right: A good look at the bare skin and "pocket" of an Adelie penguin's brood patch.

Upper Left: A hatching Adelie penguin egg. (The egg tooth, which is visible at the tip of the bill, aids the chick in breaking through the hard egg shell.)

Lower left: Downy gentoo chicks, like all penguin chicks, are fed partially digested food.

BRUSH-TAILED PENGUINS
CHAPTER FOUR

This first group of charming penguins includes the Adelie, chinstrap, and gentoo penguins. All three have distinctive long tails that sweep behind them like brooms as they walk. Adelies are truly polar and are restricted to coastal Antarctica. Chinstraps are most abundant along the Antarctic Peninsula and nearby islands. However, small groups also have colonized South Georgia Island to the north. The gentoo penguin also lives along the Antarctic Peninsula, but is more common on the subantarctic islands to the north. In some areas, all three species can be found nesting together.

The **Adelie penguin** is what most people picture in their

minds when they think of what a penguin should look like. It was named after the wife of Dumont d'Urville, the famous French naval officer and explorer.

During the Antarctic winter, Adelie penguins spend their time at sea in the pack ice.* At the approach of the southern summer, the Adelie penguins begin to move south, back to the coast. The breeding season is about to begin. By October, it is light almost twenty-four hours a day, and the penguins are

*The seasons south of the equator are just the opposite of those of the north. Therefore, the southern (or austral) winter corresponds to the northern summer (June to August). During this time, it is dark 24 hours a day.

beginning to arrive back at their ancestral rookeries. Their un-canny ability to navigate hundreds of miles and to return to the exact nesting spot of previous seasons is one of the incredible unsolved mysteries of nature.

When the Adelie penguins return, it is a very exciting time in the Antarctic. Throughout the winter, most of the animals have migrated north. Therefore, the continent is essentially lifeless — a cold and lonely place. When the penguins begin to appear at the rookeries, they trickle in, a few at a time. Then they arrive in tens, and then hundreds, and finally thousands may be arriving daily. Within weeks, the rookery, which had been as deserted as a ghost town, becomes a thriving penguin city. Life has once again returned to the Antarctic. Male Adelie penguins establish definite territories and then vigorously de-fend them. The territories are rather small, measuring approx-imately one square meter.

Once the male penguins have established their territories, they set out to attract a mate. During courtship, many different positions and calls are used. The best known is known as the Ecstatic Display. During the Ecstatic Display, the excited pen-

Previous page: A small gentoo penguin rookery in the Falkland Islands.

Right: A male Adelie penguin engaged in the Ecstatic Display.

Far right: An Adelie penguin carrying a stone to its nest.

Opposite page: Territorial disputes occasionally result in bloody battles. The incubating Adelie under the quarreling pair is not impressed.

guin points its bill to the sky while vocalizing, and at the same time slowly and rhythmically waves its flippers.

If a displaying male is successful, he will attract a mate. Remarkably, she is usually the same female of the previous season. In some colonies, the "divorce rate" is less than fifteen percent. During the courtship period, rookeries are incredibly noisy places. Human visitors sometimes find normal conversation impossible over all the racket.

Since there is no other material in the Antarctic, Adelie nests are constructed of stones. Sometimes the correct size stones are in short supply. Thus, penguins sometimes steal from one another. While a nearby pair have their backs turned, a sneaky, rock-seeking Adelie may creep over and snatch a rock. If it is caught in the act, a battle might erupt.

The nest rocks are very important. Adelie penguins often nest on steep slopes. At times, they may be four or five hundred feet above sea level and perhaps a mile from the shore. The rocks form a level platform for the eggs and keep them from rolling down the hill. The rocks also insulate the eggs from the frozen ground below.

Once the nest is completed, the birds mate. The female Adelie usually lays two pale, greenish-white eggs. Both male and female incubate, with the male taking the first turn. The female then goes to sea to feed and fatten up for the task ahead. She returns in seventeen to twenty-four days to relieve her tiring partner. By now the male has been ashore for thirty to forty days and has lost up to thirty percent of his body weight. It is now his turn to go to sea and fatten up.

The female incubates until the last week or so, when the male again takes over. Finally, after thirty-two to thirty-seven days, the eggs begin to hatch. The little Adelie chicks weigh about eighty-five grams (compared to the ten to twelve pounds for an adult), and they are very weak.

Because they must be kept warm, the chicks are brooded next to the warm skin in the brood patch. When the chicks hatch, their down is very thin. This enables the chicks to more readily absorb heat from the brooding parents. Within several weeks, a thicker down will begin to grow. By then the growing chicks are able to control their own body temperature and are

A nesting Adelie penguin with an egg. The rock nests are important because, even in the frozen Antarctic, thaws sometimes occur. If the nest is not high enough, it could be flooded out and the eggs lost. During some years, eggs and chick losses of this type can be surprisingly high. These penguins also often nest on slopes, there the rocks form a level platform which prevents the eggs from rolling away.

not nearly so dependent on the adults.

Both parents feed the chicks. At first, the little Adelie chicks are fed small amounts quite often. As they get larger, they require more and more food, but not as frequently. For the first three weeks or so after hatching, the chicks are attended, or guarded, constantly by one of the adults. This period is known as the "guard stage." The chicks require this attention not only to keep them warm, but also to protect them from skuas.

Skuas are predatory gull-like birds that are very fond of Adelie penguin chicks and eggs. Sometimes a pair of skuas may operate as a team. While one skua distracts a penguin on the nest from the front, the other will steal an egg or chick from the rear.

Some people consider this to be cruel. However, it is merely nature's way of controlling population sizes. Consider for a moment: if all eggs hatched and all chicks survived, the penguin population explosion would be enormous. In the case of a million-bird colony (500,000 pairs) the population would double in a single season. As a result, the penguins could eat

Upper left: A newly hatched Adelie penguin.

Lower left: Skuas are predatory gull-like birds. They are mainly scavengers but sometimes prey upon penguin eggs and chicks. However, many of the chicks taken by the skuas tend to be sick or weak and would probably perish anyway.

themselves out of existence. In other words, a population must be kept in balance. So, simply stated, some must die in order that most might survive. Up to 60 percent of Adelie chicks may perish before even reaching independence.

By the time the Adelie chicks are approximately three weeks old, they begin to band together in unattended groups known as créches. By collecting together, the chicks can offer one another protection. There is safety in numbers. When it gets too cold, the chicks huddle together. However, the greatest advantage of a créche-type arrangement is that it enables both adults to go to sea at the same time to feed. The growing chicks are always hungry and require more and more food, and it takes both parents to satisfy the demand.

Once the créches are formed, the Adelie chicks are off their territories but remain in the vicinity. Returning adults feed only their own young. The chicks and parents recognize one another by voice. Considering that thousands of chicks may be present, this is a remarkable feat.

When the bright sun is shining, the downy chicks tend to overheat, even when the temperature is below freezing. Dark objects absorb the sun's heat, and the dark down is very thick. Then the hot chicks pant to cool down. At times an adult will stand alongside to offer some shade. The chicks tire easily and, after being fed, often collapse on the ground and sleep.

As the chicks grow larger, increasing amounts of food are required. Sometimes when an adult returns, numerous chicks rush out to meet it. The adult will then run away with the chicks in hot pursuit. This is called a feeding chase. Since the adult will only feed its own young, the other chicks soon lose interest and fall behind. However, the chicks of that particular parent do not give up. When the adult stops, the insistent young are immediately begging for food.

By the end of their sixth week, the chicks are losing much down. They are now beginning to look more like penguins. The down does not always fall off evenly, and the chicks may look a little strange, with tufts of down poking out here and there. Sometimes only a patch is left on the top of the head, and the

Upper left: Overheated chicks often pant to cool off. This four-week old Adelie chick is obviously uncomfortable.

Upper right: The chicks tire easily and often collapse exhausted on the ground.

Lower left: At approximately three weeks of age, Adelie chicks begin to gather in groups called créches.

Lower right: Molting Adelie chicks in a feeding chase.

penguins look as they just had a "Mohawk" haircut. By February, the young Adelie penguins are almost eight weeks old, and are fully feathered.

Fledging time is very risky for juvenile penguins. They must go to the sea for the first time and learn to feed themselves. At first, they are very hesitant to enter the water. Because they are inexperienced, they do not recognize the danger of a leopard seal, and many are eaten. However, most survive. The adults, in the meantime, begin their molt. When finished, they too will return to the sea and begin migrating north to spend the winter. Thus, the cycle is completed.

Third largest of all penguins, **gentoo penguins** stand thirty-two inches tall and weigh up to fourteen pounds. They are the most docile and timid of the penguins. It is sometimes possible to handle their eggs or chicks without being attacked.

Right: A partially molted Adelie chick, approximately 7 weeks of age. When they are fledged, the youngsters will resemble their parents, except that their throats are white rather than black.

Opposite page: A gentoo penguin with two half-grown chicks. This species feeds mainly on krill, squid and fish and is capable of diving to depths of at least 300 feet in search of food.

The name gentoo apparently originated with the inhabitants of the Falkland Islands. The sealers, who were very fond of their eggs, often referred to them as Johnny penguins. But no one really seems to know why these particular names were given.

Their distribution is widespread, and thus their habitat is much more varied than it is for the other two brush-tailed penguins. Often the rookeries are located some distance from the shore, perhaps a mile or more. To reach the rookeries, the penguins usually use well-worn trails. These pathways may extend over bluffs, through valleys, and across streams and can also wind through thick tussock grass.

Gentoo rookeries are usually located on level or gently sloping terrain. Colonies may consist of just a few birds or hundreds; sometimes thousands. Gentoos are not nearly as colonial as the Adelie penguin. Their nests are often scattered.

Above: Nesting gentoos with whale bones in the background.

Middle: A gentoo with three chicks.

Below: A chinstrap penguin on the nest with a chick and an egg.

And they do not always return to the same rookery. At times, the whole colony will move to a new site.

Depending on the terrain, nests may be constructed of rocks, molted tail feathers, grass, moss, twigs, seaweed, or other vegetation. They may even contain the bleached bones of fallen comrades. As a rule, gentoo nests are much larger than those of the Adelie. Like the Adelies, gentoos may steal nest material from one another.

Much of their breeding behavior is like that of the Adelie. However, I have observed some pairs with three large chicks in the nest. Presumably, if the weather remains mild and the food supply abundant, gentoo parents are capable of rearing three young. Even so, I suspect this is a rare occurrence. Juveniles resemble adults except they are slimmer, have shorter tails and their bills are much paler in color.

The **chinstrap penguin** is named for the conspicuous black stripe across its chin. Some folks know them as ringed or bearded penguins. Their calls are earsplitting. This may be the source for yet another of their descriptive common names — the stone cracker. These bold penguins stand about twenty-seven inches tall, and large ones weigh about ten pounds.

All penguins have definite personalities. Chinstraps are fiesty by nature and are very aggressive. In fact, it is said of the three types of brush-tailed penguins that gentoos turn tail when threatened, Adelies stand their ground, but chinstraps charge. They may hiss or even growl when irritated, sometimes going so far as to stamp their feet.

Chinstrap rookeries are enormous, with the birds numbering in the millions. Indeed, one colony is said to exceed fourteen million penguins. Some biologists suggest that in recent years the population has increased. Other biologists suggest that due to the difficulty in obtaining accurate census figures, the early estimates may have been incorrect.

Some of the chinstrap rookeries are located on unbelievably rough and steep terrain. One colony at Deception Island is on a slope so steep it is difficult even for a human to climb. Some naturalists refer to the chinstraps as the alpinists, or mountain climbers, of the penguins. It is clear that penguins in general are not the delicate little creatures they are frequently made out to be.

Breeding chinstraps arrive ashore several weeks later than the Adelie and may use the same rookeries. Some of the tough little newcomers may actually chase Adelies from their nests and take over the site.

The newly hatched chinstrap chicks are a beautiful silver-gray color, but as they get older, they become rather brownish.

The chicks grow slightly faster than the Adelies and may fledge about the same time. Unlike the other brush-tailed penguins, the young do not band together into créches.

After the breeding season, the migratory chinstraps return to the sea. Little is known of their movements at that time, but they presumably move north at winter's approach. I have been privileged to see them many times far out to sea, riding picturesque icebergs.

Opposite page, above: Several chinstraps engaged in the Ecstatic Display.

Left: A chinstrap penguin with two half-grown chicks.

Below: Penguins often use icebergs to rest on when at sea. The penguins on the top of this berg are more than 80 feet from the water.

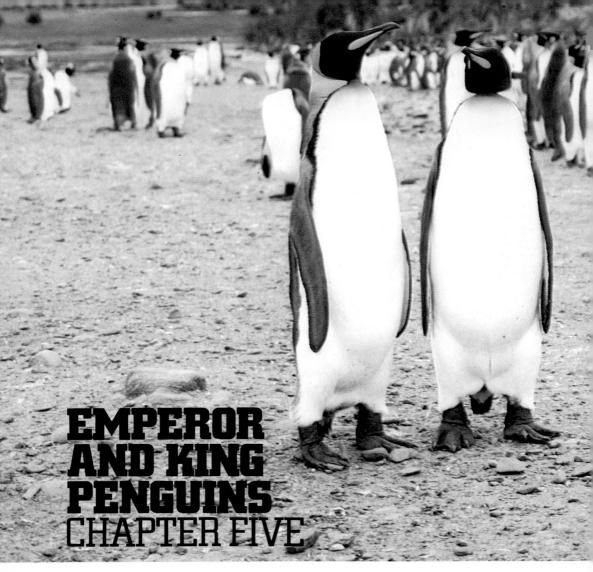

EMPEROR AND KING PENGUINS
CHAPTER FIVE

These two colorful species are the giants of the penguin world. Emperors stand in excess of three and a half feet tall and can weigh ninety or more pounds. This makes them among the largest of all birds. The forty-pound kings are smaller and less bulky, but are still quite large as far as most birds go. Brilliant gold or yellow ear patches considerably brighten up the dark heads of both species. Many people consider these two the most handsome of the penguins. And, in a number of ways, they are the most interesting.

Like the Adelie penguin of chapter four, the majestic **emperor penguin** is restricted to the Antarctic. However, the two

species share few similarities. While the Adelie is a hyperactive little creature, constantly in motion, the stately emperor typically moves slowly and deliberately. If the Adelies are the comics of the Antarctic, the dignified, peaceful emperors must certainly be the aristocrats.

No bird has a lifestyle as fascinating as that of the emperor penguin. They are winter nesters — when it is dark twenty-four hours a day. Temperatures may plunge to 80°F below zero, and the wind may howl at 120 miles per hour. Were it not for the presence of the nesting emperors, the hostile Antarctic continent would be lifeless.

Emperor penguins breed on the annual sea or fast ice.* Therefore, they may never set foot on land — the only bird with such a distinction. In April and May, the huge birds begin the long, difficult trek over the sea ice to traditional coastal rookeries. Sometimes this relatively flat ice may extend out from the continent a hundred or more miles. This is a tremendous distance for an aquatic, short-legged animal to have to walk. However, the determined emperors toboggan for much of the distance. This is much easier than walking — and certainly much faster.

Courtship begins as soon as they reach the rookeries. The frigid air is filled with the beautiful trumpeting calls of the emperors. Once the pair bond is formed, the female lays a single large white egg, which weighs slightly less than a pound. She then passes the egg to her mate, who quickly scoops it up on his feet and covers it with a loose fold of abdominal, or stomach, skin. Emperor penguins not only do not establish territories, they build no nests.

Once the male assumes custody of the egg, the female retraces her steps back to open water. The males are left alone

*Sea ice, also known as fast ice, is produced annually as the surface of the ocean freezes. This ice consists of salt water and may be 10 to 15 feet thick. During the antarctic summer, it usually breaks up, forming ice floes and pack ice. Annual sea ice is very different from icebergs. Icebergs are composed of fresh water. As the leading edges of glaciers or ice sheets break off, icebergs are calved. Ice shelves are much thicker than sea ice and may be 1,000 or more feet thick.

to incubate in an upright position for the next two months. During the frequent blizzards they huddle together in large groups to break the wind and keep warm. Since they can shuffle about with the egg balanced on their feet, there is a continual struggle to get to the interior of the huddle where it is the warmest.

Emperor penguins are very determined to keep their precious eggs warm. Nevertheless, some eggs do get jarred loose and quickly freeze. If a male loses his egg, he usually abandons the rookery and departs for open water. Nevertheless, the urge to incubate is very strong. Abandoned eggs and even bits of ice are often accepted by broody birds. (In captivity, a king penguin went as far as to incubate a hot-dog bun for several weeks.)

Incredible as it may seem, the females return to their mates in August — just about the time the chicks are due to hatch. They obviously have very accurate biological clocks. Their mates are apparently recognized by their voices. Once the fat, well-fed females arrive, they assume the domestic responsibilities.

Previous page: Courting king penguins.

Opposite page: Emperor penguins walking and tobogganning along the ice edge. Tobagganing is a very efficient way to move over smooth ice.

Above: An emperor penguin family on the move.

By this time, the males have been without food for three to four months and may have lost up to fifty percent of their total body weight. Immediately, they head out over the ice to the open water to feed and fatten up. The reader should bear in mind that due to the distance to open water, much travel time is required. This is why only the male incubates. By placing the total incubation burden on only one partner of the pair, the other is in prime condition when the chicks hatch. The production of the large egg demands a great deal of energy from the female. So the male is the obvious choice for the incubation chores.

In my opinion, there are few baby animals that are as appealing as an emperor penguin chick. Its white mask and black cap is quite unlike the pattern of any other penguin chick. In some respects, its face is rather owl-like. And, it has a very musical shrill whistle, which can be heard for a considerable distance.

The chicks are carried about on the top of the parents' feet and are covered with the belly skin, just like the egg. When they become a little larger, they ride about with only their heads poking out. The little penguins grow rapidly and soon become

Above, left: Emperor chicks are brooded on the top of their parents feet.
Above, right: Like the adults, resting chicks keep their feet off the ice in order to conserve heat.

too large to take advantage of such a unique form of transportation. But they still readily seek the warmth and security offered by the feet and loose skin. As a result, only their rear ends may be visible protruding from under the tolerant parent.

Like the Adelie penguins, the chicks tend to gather together in groups, or créches, as they increase in size. If it gets too cold, the chicks will form tight huddles to keep warm. The adults feed only their own chicks and locate them by voice.

By October, summer is close at hand. The sea ice is now breaking up. In fact, the ice edge may now be close to the rookery. Therefore, feeding adults do not have to travel far to reach open water. Some years, however, tragedy strikes. If the ice breaks up prematurely, the rookery will be destroyed. If the chicks are still in down, they could all be lost. Severe blizzards can also account for extensive chick mortality.

By January, the chicks are four to five months old and are ready to fledge. It is now easy to understand why the emperor penguin breeds during the middle of the Antarctic winter. In January the weather is most pleasant; open water is nearby and the food supply is abundant. This is the ideal time for the young birds strike out on their own. Since it takes two months to

When it gets cold, emperor chicks huddle together in a compact group. The chicks on the outer edge of the huddle tend to try to work themselves in to the center of the group where it is warmest.

hatch an egg and at least four months to rear a chick, the emperors must begin to breed in June if young are to reach independence by January.

At first glance, the striking **king penguin** appears to be a small emperor penguin. It is true that they share a number of similarities, but in many ways they are quite different. King penguins inhabit a number of the vegetation-covered subantarctic islands. The climate there is not nearly as severe as it is in the Antarctic. As a result, breeding king penguins do not have to put up with the drastic seasonal extremes that the emperors must face.

The breeding arrangement of the king penguin is every bit as strange as that of the emperor. They do not breed on annual sea ice. (There is none.) Traditional shore-based rookeries are used. These may be rather muddy and untidy. Some of the colonies can be large, consisting of tens of thousands of penguins. A king penguin establishes a definite territory, but this is usually only the size of the ground it is standing on.

The single, pear-shaped egg is incubated in the same way as that of an emperor. However, both parents take turns incubating. They can do this because open water is close at hand. Remember, open water is required for feeding. The fact that both parents incubate may be the reason a territory is required. This would make it easier for the returning bird to

Opposite page: Few animals are as appealing as emperor penguin chicks.

Left: A crèche of emperor chicks. Leaving the downy chicks unattended enables both parents to feed at the same time.

locate its mate.

After fifty-two to fifty-six days, the eggs hatch. The little king chicks are not nearly as appealing as those of the emperor. As the chicks grow, they become covered with a very thick, brownish down. The down is so long that it looks like hair blowing in the wind. In fact, large chicks are so "hairy" that early observers sometimes referred to them as "wooly penguins".*

Incredibly, it may take a pair of adults ten to thirteen months to fledge a chick. During the winter, when food is scarce and they are fed irregularly, the fat chicks may have to depend exclusively on their blubber for weeks at a time.

Because of their extremely long rearing period, king penguins can only produce two chicks within a three-year period. On the other hand, emperor penguins breed every year. When fledging time approaches, the king chicks begin to shed their long down. Wispy patches of down, spread randomly over the bird, are not uncommon. Soon all the down is lost, and the juveniles are on their own.

Right: A king penguin rookery.

Opposite page, Upper left: An incubating king penguin.

Upper right: King penguin chicks are not nearly as attractive as emperor chicks.

Lower left: A large king penguin chick.

Lower right: While the downy chicks hardly resemble the adults, an unbelieveable transformation begins once their molt starts.

*Down, while it may resemble hair or wool, is actually a modified feather.

CRESTED PENGUINS
CHAPTER SIX

This flashy group of comical penguins is named for its fancy orange or yellow crests. They also have distinct fiery-red eyes. The various species are similar in appearance but can be distinguished by the size, shape, and color of the crest and bill. Most crested penguins inhabit remote subantarctic islands, but some live alongside humans, particularly in New Zealand and the Falkland Islands.

The rockhopper is the best known of the crested penguins. And the macaroni is known to many people. The royal penguin is identical to the macaroni, except its throat is white rather than black. The remaining three crested penguins — the Snares

Island, Fiordland, and erect-crested penguins — are little known and live in the waters around southern New Zealand and surrounding islands. Like the royal penguins, they have very restricted ranges. In fact, the entire population of two to three million royal penguins breeds *only* at Macquarie Island.

Male and female crested penguins look essentially alike, although the males are slightly more robust, and their bills are significantly larger. The pair bonds are quite strong, and the birds may reoccupy the same nesting territory as the previous season.

The crested penguins occupy a variety of different habitats.

The Fiordland crested penguin, for example, might be encountered in the coastal rain forest. And, the Snares Island penguin may actually roost in low trees. Some occupy steep rocky cliffs. As a group, crested penguins may spend more time continuously at sea than any of the other penguins — up to five months.

Crested penguins are rather unusual in a number of ways. They typically lay two eggs. But curiously, the first is always significantly smaller than the second — as much as twenty to fifty percent smaller. Both eggs are generally fertile, and both may hatch. But rarely, if ever, do both chicks survive.

The **rockhopper penguin** is the smallest of the crested penguins. However, what it lacks in size it more than makes up for in temperament. Standing only fifteen to twenty-two inches tall and weighing a mere five and a half pounds, these little birds have the reputation of being the most aggressive of all penguins, the males even more so than their mates. This reputation is well deserved.

The fearless, bad-tempered rockhoppers will readily attack any unsuspecting intruder that wanders into the rookery, even if that intruder is human. In fact, they can become so enraged at the disturbance that they may actually jump up

Previous page: Rockhopper penguins.

Above: A Fiordland crested penguin on its nest in the coastal rain forest of southern New Zealand.

Above: Royal penguins with a chick.

Lower left: A family of erect-crested penguins.

Lower right: A courting pair of Snares Island crested penguins.

and grasp a pant leg with their bills. Then, hanging on like a nasty little dog, they painfully smack the leg with their rock-hard, bony flippers. Even when the leg is vigorously shaken, the little penguins doggedly hang on. Sometimes two, or even three, will grab on at the same time.

Their bills are razor sharp and are powerful weapons, well designed for slashing and tearing. The belligerent penguins do not hesitate to bite and can easily draw blood. Based on my own experience, I would rather take on a ninety-pound emperor penguin than a fiesty rockhopper.

Their descriptive common name, rockhopper, accurately describes their manner of locomotion when ashore. With both

feet held together, they bounce like ping-pong balls over rocks. One biologist suggested that rockhoppers looked rather like children engaged in a sack race.

Ashore, rockhoppers are the most agile of the penguins. They are able to move over some of the roughest terrain imaginable. And they do it with ease. Sometimes, when going down steep cliffs, the little penguins may jump four to five feet to the next ledge. From time to time, I have seen them fall ten feet or more to the rocks below. Always, they bounced up immediately and hopped away without apparent harm. Most penguin species dive into the water. Rockhoppers, however, often jump in feet first.

Opposite page: Considered by many people to be among the most attractive of birds, rockhoppers have bright yellow crests which sweep back over their distinctive red eyes. The crest forms beautiful drooping tassels on either side of the head. While they have a variety of calls, the most typical is a loud, throbbing bray which can be considered obnoxious.

Left: A rockhopper penguin rookery. At this stage, the chicks are beginning to form créches.

Their breeding sites are frequently located on incredibly steep hillsides. Just getting there can be a major chore. Rockhoppers tend to use well-defined penguin trails. At times, these trails wind up the steep rock slopes over large boulders. The trails have been used for so many generations that the rocks are scarred and grooved. Even rock is no match for millions of little penguin feet passing over it for centuries.

Some rockhopper colonies are huge, containing hundreds of thousands of penguins. During the courtship period, the rookeries are very noisy. The sounds can be heard for miles.

Rockhoppers establish and fiercely defend territories. The nest is usually a depression in the ground, which may be lined with sticks, vegetation, stones, and even molted feathers. In some regions they may use caves or burrows. Both sexes incubate for thirty-two to thirty-five days. The little chicks are brownish with conspicuous whitish bellies. Like some of the other penguins, the young begin to band together in crèches at about three weeks of age. After some sixty-seven to seventy-two days, the juveniles reach independence.

Rockhoppers are highly migratory, and after the breeding season they return to the sea. While at sea, their lifestyle is largely mysterious. The adults may come back to the rookery within a month or so to molt. After that, they are not seen again until the following breeding season, when once again they appear at the rookeries.

Much larger in size than the rockhoppers, **macaroni penguins** stand twenty-eight inches tall and weigh nine pounds. Their crests are vivid orange rather than yellow. In the old days, some English gentlemen were known for a bizarre hairstyle known as a Macaroni coiffure. When sailors first saw the penguins, they were instantly reminded of the dandies and their peculiar hairstyle. Thus this species became known as the macaroni penguin.

These birds are among the most colonial of all penguins, perhaps even of all birds. The sheer number of penguins in some rookeries is beyond belief. Unlike an Adelie penguin colony, breeding macaroni penguins form a single solid mass — a colorful living carpet of penguins. On South Georgia Island alone, millions upon millions assemble in massive rookeries.

Macaroni rookeries may be located on even rougher terrain than those of the rockhoppers. To reach them, one almost has to be a mountain goat. (Curiously, some people suggest these penguins even smell like goats.) Were it not for the fact that the penguins were actually climbing the steep rocky slopes, the feat would be considered impossible. I can clearly recall one rookery in particular I climbed to. The vertical rocks were very slippery and covered with ice and snow. It was one of the most hair-raising, and perhaps stupid, things I have ever done.

Macaroni breeding behavior parallels that of the rockhopper. At about two months of age, the macaroni chicks fledge; usually in January or February. The adults also go to sea at that time to fatten up. A month or so later, they return to the rookery to molt. Millions of penguins molting at the same time and place drop billions of feathers. My first reaction upon seeing such a spectacle was that I had come upon the aftermath of the world's greatest pillow fight.

Above, left: Macaroni penguins just prior to their molt. Notice their long drooping orange crests.

Above, right: During the molt, macaroni penguin feathers cover the ground. When the wind blows, the scene looks like a violent snowstorm.

YELLOW-EYED AND FAIRY PENGUINS
CHAPTER SEVEN

Yellow-eyed penguins are obviously named for their bright yellow, cat-like eyes. They also have a beautiful, pale sulphur-yellow crown. These are fairly large penguins, and a fat one might weigh more than thirteen pounds. They stand just over two feet in height.

Essentially a southern New Zealand species, yellow-eyed penguins also breed on some of the other nearby islands. They may even nest near cities. Dogs and other predators can be troublesome. But the penguins are usually capable of defending themselves. If a nosey dog ventures too close, the defensive penguin may call loudly and then smack it with a powerful

flipper. This generally discourages all but the most persistent intruders.

Unlike the penguins discussed in previous chapters, yellow-eyed penguins do not assemble in large colonies, nor are they migratory. They are usually seen in small groups or,once in a while, even as a single breeding pair. In addition, they are quite wary and tend to move away when people are near.

Yellow-eyed penguin nesting sites are varied and scattered and may be located in the tall tussock grass, low forest, or under large rocks. Sometimes they dig burrows. I even encountered one pair nesting in an abandoned shed. The nests typically have a strong smell. The breeding season extends from August to May. However, eggs are generally laid only from late September to early October.

The two eggs are incubated by both partners. The incubation period may exceed forty days. They commonly successfully rear two chicks. This takes between 110 and 115 days. Chicks usually fledge in February.

We don't know how long penguins live. But, at least in the case of yellow-eyed penguins, birds known to be at least twenty years old have been seen with chicks. (Some penguins in zoos have survived for more than thirty years.)

Smallest of all the penguins, **fairy penguins** are often referred to as little blue penguins because of their bluish color. They are tiny compared to their larger relatives. Weighing only two and a half pounds, they stand about sixteen inches. It would take more than thirty of them to equal the weight of a single emperor penguin. They occur both in New Zealand and Australia. They tend not to migrate.

Because they live so close to civilization, the little fairy

penguins experience some problems not faced by other penguin species. As strange as it may sound, a number are actually run over by cars as they cross roads. Others are killed by fisherman and used as bait in lobster traps, even though they are legally protected.

Nature can also be harsh. Severe winter storms can cause extensive mortality. And predators are always on the prowl. Pacific gulls, water rats, cats, dogs, ferrets, large lizards, and even tiger snakes must be avoided.

Fairy penguins are quite agile when ashore. They are also surprisingly capable climbers and can scramble up rather steep cliffs using their bills, flippers, and feet. They are very vocal, especially at night. Their calls include a wide variety of unusual sounds: growling, screaming, quacking, trumpeting, mooing, braying, cackling, hissing, bleating, sneezing, barking, and even meowing rather like a cat.

During the day, they either spend their time in burrows or at sea. Fairy penguins are the most nocturnal of the penguins. Shortly after dark, they begin to come ashore. At Phillip Island, near the city of Melbourne, Australia, crowds of people gather

Previous page: A yellow-eyed penguin.

Opposite page, left: Yellow-eyed penguins are not nearly as social as some of the other penguins and may be found alone along the coast.

Opposite page, right: A yellow-eyed penguin on its nest between two large boulders.

Left: Smallest of the penguins, fairy penguins are also known as blue penguins because of their color.

in the evening and eagerly await the penguin parade. Flood-lights have been set up, but the penguins have gotten used to all the attention. Much to the delight of the onlookers, the penguins carry on as if no one was there. The spectacle has become quite a famous attraction.

Fairy penguin nesting sites are quite variable. The birds may nest as close to the sea as the high tide line or as far as a mile inland. Sometimes they form colonies, but isolated pairs are not uncommon either. Although they do nest on the mainland, they tend to prefer offshore islands. The islands, of course, offer much more protection from predators and human disturbance.

Although they most often burrow, fairy penguins may also

Upper right: A fairy penguin incubating in its underground burrow. At times, the nest site may be located up rather steep cliffs. These little penguins are surprisingly capable climbers and when moving up steep banks, use their bills and flippers to help with the climb.

Lower right: A fairy penguin chick just prior to fledging.

Opposite page: A fairy penguin family at the entrance to their nesting burrow.

nest in rock crevices or under thick vegetation. On occasion, they may even nest under a house. They are not always welcome when they select such an unusual nesting site. Their loud calls have already been mentioned; and they call mostly at night. You can easily imagine how difficult it would be to sleep with a noisy pair of courting penguins in the basement.

If the ground is soft enough, the penguins dig their own burrows. Some burrows may be quite long — up to five feet. At times, the penguins may take over and enlarge a petrel burrow. Nesting underground provides a great deal of protection and security for the little penguins.

Fairy penguin eggs are generally laid between July and November. Both parents incubate the two rather large white eggs for thirty-eight to forty days. The chicks are attended by at least one parent until they are about three weeks old. At that time, the young are left alone in the burrows during the day. The parents return at night to feed them. When they are about a month old, the chicks begin to come out of the burrow to wait for the parents and their meal.

At about eight weeks of age, the chicks are fully feathered. The parents then abandon them, and the juveniles are on their own. Often, both chicks survive to the fledging stage. Sometimes fairy penguins will nest again and may rear more than two chicks in the same year. This is quite unusual in the kingdom of penguins.

WARM-WEATHER PENGUINS
CHAPTER EIGHT

Since these penguins inhabit the coasts of South America and South Africa, they are essentially warm-climate penguins. Thus, they are the ones most commonly seen in zoos, because they are the easiest to maintain in captivity. All four warm-weather species have very distinct donkey-like braying calls. The South African birds sound so much like braying donkeys that they are more commonly known as jackass penguins. All four species nest underground.

The **Magellanic penguin** is by far the most numerous of this group of penguins. In fact, the famous colony at Punta Tumbo in Argentina is home for a million or more birds. The

species also occurs in southern Chile and the Falkland Islands.

These penguins are quite variable in habitat preference and temperment, depending on where they live. The Magellanic penguins that breed on the mainland in Argentina tend to be extremely colonial and may form large, densely packed colonies. In the Falklands, this is not the case. While a hundred or so pairs may nest in the same area, it is not uncommon to find isolated groups of only four or five pairs nesting, and the nests may be widely scattered.

In the Falkland Islands, Magellanic penguins may be seen in the company of rockhopper and gentoo penguins.

Compared to the rockhoppers, they are very shy. If approached too closely, they tend to either dash into the surf or rapidly scoot down their burrows.

Magellanic penguins nest underground, generally in burrows they dig themselves. The holes can be quite deep, particuarly when they burrow into soft earth. The nest chamber is large enough to accommodate both adults. In areas with many nests, a human visitor must step carefully. If not, the top of a burrow might cave in because of the weight.

Because they nest underground, all warm-weather penguins are much more difficult to study than the species that nest in the open. To weigh and measure eggs or chicks, I have often been forced to reach far down into a black hole to reach them. The defensive adults were not impressed with my scientific curiosity. Magellanic penguins have powerful stout bills, which are very sharp indeed. Their slashing bites are most painful and always draw blood.

Reaching down into a darkened burrow quickly demonstrates the security offered by the holes. A predator sneaking down a hole would come face to face with an incubating or brooding adult. Based on my own experience, I suspect that few predators attempt it more than once.

As a rule, two white eggs are laid. These are incubated by

both parents for thirty-nine to forty-three days. Upon hatching, the little Magellanic chicks are blind and helpless. Since the chicks and adults remain in contact by voice, sight is not required at first in a dark burrow. But within a week or so, their eyes are open.

Compared to some of the other penguins, this species requires a great deal of time to rear a chick — up to three months. Upon reaching independence, the juveniles are smaller than the adults, duller in color, and lack the facial pattern.

By far the most familiar of the zoo penguins, the **Humboldt penguin**, is sometimes called the Peruvian penguin. Since its survival is dependent on the fertile cool Humboldt Current, which flows northward along the west coast of South America, the name Humboldt is perhaps more appropriate. These birds

Previous page: A flock of Humboldt penguins.

Opposite page: Magellanic penguins may dig burrows five feet or more in length in soft soil. In some areas, heavy rains flood out many burrows causing high egg and chick losses.

Left: The jackass-like calls of the Magellanic penguins are typical of the warm weather penguins. This species is by far the most numerous of the group, as its population exceeds a million individuals.

are restricted to Peru and Chile. Like the Magellanic penguins, they weigh about ten pounds and stand just over two feet tall. Rather timid and shy birds, they are seldom seen in large groups.

This species may be in real trouble. No early population size estimates are available, but Humboldt penguins formerly were regarded as "extremely abundant." Some biologists believe they are declining; perhaps no more than ten thousand currently exist. Clearly, the Humboldt penguin may already be an endangered species. There are undoubtedly a number of factors responsible for the apparently drastic population decline. The cool, nutrient-laden waters of the Humboldt Current formerly supported countless tons of anchovies. These sardine-like fish are the birds' main food. In recent years, however, the area has been overfished by Peruvian fishermen. With less food available, seabird populations tend to decline.

However, there is perhaps a greater threat. The guano, or droppings, of fish-eating birds dries to form a white powder. On some of the nesting islands to the west of Peru, millions of seabirds concentrate to breed: mainly cormorants, pelicans, boobies, and penguins. Over the years, the compacted guano deposits accumulated to 150 or more feet thick. The guano could easily be burrowed into and was therefore essential to the nesting penguins.

Unfortunately for the penguins, guano is one of the richest fertilizers known to man. Thus, it was mined and formed a basis for a billion-dollar industry. Between 1848 and 1875 alone,

Opposite page: Although similar to Magellanic penguins in many ways, Humboldt penguins have only one black chest stripe instead of two.

Left: A Humboldt penguin chick in its burrow. The burrow offers security and cool relief from the hot sun.

more than 20 million *tons* were exported. With the guano scraped down to bare rock in many areas, the penguins had no place to nest. If reproduction is significantly reduced, a population will sooner or later begin to dwindle.

Also known as the jackass penguins, **black-footed penguins** live on islands off the tip of South Africa. Slightly smaller than their South American cousins, they too appear to be suffering. As recently as 1967, it was a common practice to harvest and sell their eggs. Between 1900 and 1930, almost half a million eggs were collected annually from a single colony alone.

In addition, predators such as kelp gulls and sacred ibis can take up to forty percent of the eggs. The threat of a major oil spill is also a source of great concern. Some spills have already occurred. Huge supertankers commonly sail around South Africa. A single major oil spill could result in the loss of thousands of penguins and other marine creatures.

One of the most famous black-footed penguin colonies is located on Dassen Island. It was said that millions formerly nested there. Today, this colony has been reduced to only 70,000 penguins. In 1972, it was estimated that the *total* population of black-footed penguins was only 170,000 birds. This figure represents but ten percent of their former numbers.

Considered by some to be the most attractive of the warm weather penguins, black-footed penguins also nest under-

ground in burrows they dig themselves. The cooler underground cavities offer some relief from the hot African sun. Or they may nest between boulders or other sheltered sites. If they can get away with it, they will steal nesting material from their neighbors. Some pairs may nest twice a year.

The little, rather dull-colored **Galapagos penguin** lives farther north than any other penguin species. The Galapagos Islands lie just south of the equator — approximately six hundred miles to the west of Ecuador. But even these sun-baked islands are noted for the presence of constant cool-water current.

Smallest of the tropical penguins, these little birds weigh only five pounds and are less than two feet tall. They are seldom observed in large groups. Thirty to forty in the same area would be considered a fairly large number.

Their numerical status has long been controversial, and they are officially considered endangered. Population estimates have ranged between 500 and 15,000 birds. Detailed recent research suggests that 15,000 is probably more accurate. It is probable that the population has never been larger than this. The existing habitat may not be able to support a greater number of Galapagos penguins. If so, they are not really endangered at all. But in order to assure continued survival, they must be totally protected, because they are very vulnerable.

Opposite page: A group of black-footed penguins. These penguins nest underground and line their burrows with old feathers, vegetation, bits of dried seaweed, or other rubbish.

Left: Two Galapagos penguins. To keep cool during the day, these penguins spend their time either at sea or in the shade of volcanic rock.

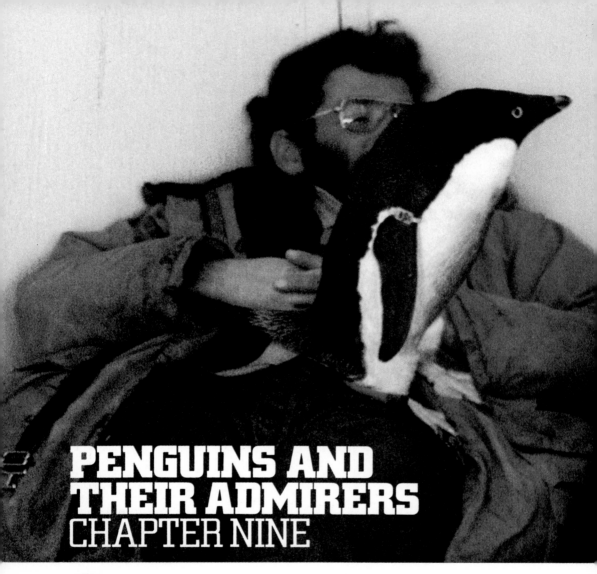

PENGUINS AND THEIR ADMIRERS
CHAPTER NINE

One of the first statements made about penguins at the beginning of this book was that they are undoubtedly among the most popular of all zoo animals. This has been the case for more than a hundred years. Why then, don't we see more penguins in zoos?

Because penguins are such specialized animals, they can be difficult to keep in zoos. This is particularly true of the polar species, which require special enclosed, refrigerated exhibits. The more tropical birds are much easier to maintain and, hence, are more common in zoos. Fortunately for the penguins, and for us, a great deal has been learned in recent years. As a

result, penguins in captivity are in better health and are surviving longer than before.

In the past, penguins were considered very difficult to breed in captivity. Few zoos had much success, but there were exceptions. The wonderful, prolific colony of gentoos at the Edinburgh Zoo in Scotland is perhaps the most famous. In North America, a number of zoos have begun to concentrate more and more on breeding their penguins. The St. Louis, Detroit, Milwaukee, Montreal, and Baltimore zoos, to name but a few, have all been successful in their efforts.

However, until the early 1970's very little had been

accomplished with the polar species. In 1973, Sea World, the Hubbs/Sea World Research Institute, and the National Science Foundation joined forces in an attempt to establish a breeding colony of Adelie and emperor penguins in San Diego, California. The main purpose of the colony was to facilitate long-term research.

At first, the Sea World field team worked in the Antarctic for several seasons to study the penguins in the wild. During this time, the techniques required to maintain the birds in San Diego were developed.

Adult pairs of Adelie penguins were collected at the Cape Crozier rookery on Ross Island, some two thousand miles south of New Zealand. The penguins were then flown by Navy helicopter to a special enclosure prepared for them at the McMurdo Research Station. To keep track of who was who, all birds were banded. Each pair had its own number. Males were banded on the right flipper and females on the left.

Individual emperor penguins were collected along the ice edge. Normally gentle and docile creatures, they were very powerful and difficult for us to handle once they were restrained. Catching penguins is not for the faint of heart.

To make the long flight from the Antarctic back to the United States, an Air Force C-141 was used. The temperature inside the plane was kept below zero in order to make the birds more comfortable. The penguins thrived. Ultimately, several hundred penguins were successfully airlifted from the Antarctic to sunny California. In San Diego, the penguins are housed in a

Previous page: The author (right) with a field associate and three curious, but unconcerned, Adelie penguins. This photograph was taken prior to the penguin airlift from Antarctica to the United States.

Right: A portion of the gentoo penguin colony at the zoo in Edinburgh, Scotland.

Above left: Collecting the Adelies at the huge rookery at Cape Crozier. In order to increase the chances of breeding in San Diego, only mated pairs were selected.

Above right: A helicopter arriving at the penguin holding area.

Left: Restraining a powerful, struggling emperor penguin is no easy matter.

Below: Loading the penguins aboard the cargo plane. The active volcano, Mt. Erebus is smoking in the background.

very special research freezer.

In order to maintain polar penguins in prime condition, they must be always kept at subfreezing temperatures. Ice is very important and is the ideal substance for the penguins to walk on. Eight thousand pounds of ice is made daily inside the freezer. The ice is then spread out on the floor. The penguins also have two salt-water pools available, which are in constant use. The light in the research freezer is kept on the same schedule as the light in the Antarctic.

Within weeks after arrival, the penguins adjusted perfectly to their new home. But the major task was still ahead — to get them to breed. Each year in October, approximately one-third of the freezer was converted into an Adelie rookery. Tons of nesting rock were hauled in. It worked: the penguins reacted as if they had never left Antarctica. Being in the freezer with them during the breeding season was almost like returning to the Antarctic.

In the San Diego rookery, courting and calling pairs established territories, stole one another's rocks, and so forth. Eggs were laid on schedule, and many chicks were reared. All of their behavior was exactly the same as that we had seen in the wild.

In order to gain more information, we decided to hand raise some of the chicks. Therefore, one egg from each of the two egg clutches was taken and placed in a mechanical incubator. Much to our delight, many of them hatched.

To hand rear the tiny chicks, we had to develop a special formula. This was finally accomplished after much trial and error. Numerous ingredients are required for the formula and once it is prepared, it looks rather like a milkshake.

Opposite page: A look inside the research freezer at Sea World in San Diego. Most of the penguins are fed by hand, and will mob the keeper at mealtime.

Left: An Adelie chick hatching in the freezer. Note the flipper identification band on the adult penguin.

Below: Adelie eggs in the incubator.

At first the chicks were fed a little at a time. In order to keep accurate growth rates, the chicks were weighed before and after each feeding. A syringe was used to feed them. Getting them started requires a very skilled and dedicated person. Normally they were fed four times a day. Once they got started, they grew very rapidly.

When the chicks were between two and three weeks old, it was necessary to begin to cool them down. So they were moved to a chilly, air-conditioned room. Next, at about one month of age, the youngsters were transferred to the research freezer but were kept separate from the other birds. At seven or eight weeks of age, they were released. At that point, they were fully feathered and were identical to the parent-raised chicks.

Not unexpectedly, the hand-raised chicks are even more fearless than the other penguins. When the bird keepers enter the freezer, they are immediately mobbed by the excited penguins, particularly if the penguins are hungry. As of 1979, the breeding success has been most encouraging. One hundred and twelve Adelies had been reared in three years. Between

Above, left: Feeding a newly hatched chick with a syringe.

Above, right: Adelie chicks and their foster parent chatting with one another.

November and December of 1979 alone, 54 pairs laid a total of 106 eggs, of which 60 hatched and 56 were raised.

Breeding the emperor penguins proved to be much more challenging. Two infertile eggs were laid in 1979. Seven more eggs were laid the following year, and on September 16, 1980, the first chick of its kind ever to be hatched in captivity emerged. Within several days, it was joined by two others. This long-awaited event enabled researchers to accurately document early adult/chick behavior. Much of the information obtained was new and added a great deal to our current knowledge of these fascinating winter-nesting birds.

Sea World is also concentrating on breeding Humboldt penguins. Since they are in trouble in the wild, captive breeding populations are extremely important. Unlike the Antarctic penguins, the Humboldts are kept outside. In San Diego, they live in the salt water of Mission Bay. Their enclosure is very similar to their natural habitat. Just as they do in the wild, the nesting Humboldt penguins dig underground burrows.

Since the hand rearing of the Adelie penguins was so

Research requires recording a great deal of data. The weights of all chicks are written down before and after each feeding.

successful, this technique was used with the Humboldt penguins as well. It worked, and more and more are being reared each year. However, warm-weather penguins are much more difficult to hand raise than their Antarctic relatives; it takes over three months to rear one, rather than just seven or eight weeks.

Some of the hand-raised Humboldt penguins think they are people. They do not care to be with the other penguins. Instead, they would rather mingle with their foster parents, the penguin people. These particular youngsters have proved to be very

valuable research birds. They are easy to handle and will follow a keeper anywhere — like a faithful dog.

The science of "penguinology" has come a long way in zoos. The work at Sea World and other institutions clearly demonstrates that penguins can be kept and bred. Naturally this requires much hard work and very skilled animal keepers. But the penguins are worth all the effort, and we are learning more about them every day. As a result, the penguins are benefiting, and so are we.

Opposite page: The first emperor chick ever hatched outside the Antarctic. The unique method of brooding the chick on the top of the feet is clearly illustrated.

Left: A newly hatched Humboldt penguin.

Below: A penguin admirer strolling with a number of the hand-raised Humboldt penguins.

THE FUTURE
CHAPTER TEN

The world is rapidly changing — perhaps too rapidly. The continuing population explosion places enormous pressures on the environment. Many life forms have disappeared forever because of human thoughtlessness and greed. Sadly, it seems that others are likely to follow.

Fortunately, *most* penguin populations are fairly secure — at least for the moment. But there are exceptions. The plight of the Humboldt penguin was discussed in chapter eight. The population of black-footed penguins has apparently decreased by as much as ninety percent. And the small size of the Galapagos penguin population makes this species somewhat

insecure. But overall, at least in recent times, the penguins have done surprisingly well in a human-dominated world.

In earlier times, however, respect for penguins was not what it is today. Millions of eggs were harvested for human consumption. Early sailors looked upon the penguins themselves as a welcome food source. Hundreds of thousands were killed and salted down to be eaten during long sea voyages.

But the most disgusting practice of all was boiling down penguins for their oil. The profits from oil were so great that the whalers and sealers became very greedy. Once the great herds of fur seals and elephant seals were wiped out, the penguins were next. Millions of penguins were slaughtered, and even the little rockhopper penguin was said to yield as much as a pint of high-quality oil. At Macquarie Island alone, no less than 150,000 royal penguins were boiled down each year. This went on for a quarter of a century before it was finally stopped. King penguins in particular were heavily exploited for their oil, and numerous colonies were totally eliminated. Fortunately, this magnificent species has made a remarkable comeback in many areas.

I can remember one occasion on South Georgia Island that clearly illustrated past inhumanity to penguins. Upon seeing an

enormous pot, I commented that it must have been used to boil the penguins. My British companion quickly corrected me — "Oh no," he said. "The kettles were for boiling elephant seals. The penguins were used for fuel."

Fortunately, such barbaric acts are past for penguins. Today all penguin species are legally protected. But is this enough to insure their survival? I'm not so sure. There are disturbing signs that indicate the future might be even more dangerous for the penguins than the past.

Consider, for example, the Antarctic. There can be no question that this ecologically fragile continent will soon be exploited for its mineral and biological riches. The small, shrimp-like organism, krill, is very abundant in the water surrounding Antarctica. Krill is the basic food of the marine life there. Unfortunately, in a protein-starved world, humans also view it as a food source. Already some nations are harvesting krill. If harvesting is not carefully regulated, and too much krill is taken, all the other dependent creatures could suffer.

By now, we should know better. But, can we learn from the painful lessons of yesteryear? It is true that we no longer boil penguins for their oil. But we still tend to overfish the oceans. Introduced predators continue to be troublesome. Oil spills are becoming an ever-increasing threat. Invisible global contamination in the form of toxic pesticide pollution is becoming a fact of life.

Previous page: A trio of emperor penguins in the splendor of the Antarctic.

Opposite page, above: Adelie penguins on an ice ledge.

Opposite page, below: King penguins near the shore line.

Left: An Adelie penguin rookery.

Fortunately, most people genuinely care what happens to penguins — and to other life forms as well. It is hoped that good sense will prevail, and these wonderful animals will be preserved for future generations to marvel at. Most people acknowledge that they will never see penguins in the wild. But just knowing that they are there is enough.

INDEX

A

B

C

D

E

R

Reproduction. See Breeding
Research freezer, 82
Ringed penguins, 43-45
Rockhopper penguins, 59-62, 90
  see also Crested penguins
Rocks, for nests, 35
Rookeries, 27
  of Adelie penguins, 34, 35, 44, 82
  of chinstrap penguins, 43-44
  of emperor penguins, 48-51
  of gentoo penguins, 41-43
  of king penguins, 53
  of macaroni penguins, 62-63
  of Magellanic penguins, 70-71
  of rockhopper penguins, 62
Royal penguins, 56, 90

S

Sea ice, 48, 51
Sea World, San Diego, 80-87
Shape, of penguin, 22
Sight, 19-20, 73
Size, 12-13, 24
  see also individual penguins
Skuas, 37
Snares Island penguins, 56, 59
Sounds. See Calls; Voice
South Africa, 76
South America, 73, 75
South Pole, 10
Species, 16
Stone-cracker penguins, 43
Subantarctic islands, 18, 32, 53, 56
Summer, 33
Swimming, 21-22

T

Tails, 22, 32
Temperament. See Personality
Temperature, body, 23-24
Territories, 34, 53, 62
Tobogganing, 48
Trails, penguin, 41, 62

V

Vision, 19-20, 73
Voice, 38, 49, 51
  see also Calls

W

Warmbloodedness, 23
Warm-weather penguins, 24, 70-77
  see also Magellanic, Humboldt,
    black-footed, and Galapagos
    penguins
Waterproofing, 25, 26
Wings, 21-22
  see also Flippers
Winter, 33-34, 47

Y

Yellow-eyed penguins,64-66

Z

Zoos, 70, 78-79

SCIENTIFIC CLASSIFICATION

Order: *Sphenisciformes*
Family: *Spheniscidae*

Emperor penguin   *Aptenodytes forsteri*
King penguin   *A. pagatonica*
Adelie penguin   *Pygoscelis adeliae*
Gentoo penguin   *P. papua*
Chinstrap penguin   *P. antarctica*
Rockhopper penguin   *Eudyptes crestatus*
Macaroni penguin   *E. chrysolophus*
Royal penguin   *E. schlegeli*
Fiordland crested penguin
E. pachyrhynchus
Erect-crested penguin   *E. schateri*
Snares Island penguin   *E. robustus*
Yellow-eyed penguin   *Megadyptes antipodes*
Fairy (Little blue) penguin   *Eudyptula minor*
Magellanic penguin
Spheniscus magellanicus
Humboldt penguin   *S. humboldti*
Black-footed penguin   *S. demersus*
Galapagos penguin   *S. mendiculus*

BIBLIOGRAPHY

Peterson, R. T. *Penguins*. Boston:
Houghton Mifflin Co., 1979.

Sparks, S. and Soper, T. *Penguins*.
Great Britain: David and Charles,
Limited, 1967.

Stonehouse, B. *Penguins*. New
York: Golden Press, 1968.